SPECTACULAR
Space

SPECTACULAR Space

Inbali Iserles

Collins

Contents

Bonus

Timeline of space scientists

Albert Einstein
(1879–1955)
Germany

Subrahmanyan
Chandrasekhar
(1910–1995)
Pakistan

1879   1900   1910

Cecilia Payne-Gaposchkin
(1900–1979)
England

Katherine Johnson
(1918–2020)
United States

Jocelyn Bell Burnell
(born 1943)
Northern Ireland

1918   1942   1943

Stephen Hawking
(1942–2018)
England

3

CHAPTER 1
100 years in space

The universe began almost 14 billion years ago as the result of a huge explosion known as the "big bang". So 100 years is no time at all when we think of space! But in the last 100 years, we've learnt a great deal about the **galaxies** that surround us. We've discovered that nothing can travel faster than the speed of light. We've found out about black holes and pulsars, and that stars are made of different stuff to planets.

This book takes a closer look at some of the amazing scientists of the last 100 years, and how their exciting discoveries changed the way we see space.

The big bang

This is the name for the giant explosion at the beginning of the universe, about 14 billion years ago. The explosion caused tiny bits of light and energy to form atoms. Those atoms clustered as stars, comets, asteroids and planets.

Albert Einstein

Albert Einstein is probably the most famous scientist who ever lived! He was born in Germany in 1879. As a boy, he was always asking questions and trying to make sense of the world. As a young man, Einstein studied maths and science in Switzerland.

In 1905, when he was in his twenties, Einstein came up with his first big idea, "special relativity". In 1915, he shared his next big idea, "general relativity".

Einstein's ideas amazed other scientists because they were new ways of looking at the universe. Before Einstein, scientists thought that some things are just true and don't change, like the speed that things move or the way that gravity works. Einstein disagreed!

Gravity

Gravity is the force that pulls one thing to another thing. On Earth, gravity stops us from floating into the sky. It also means that if you drop a plate, it will crash to the floor!

Einstein's ideas about relativity are very complicated. Not many people understand them! But here are a couple of his interesting ideas:

Special relativity

Einstein discovered that nothing – not even something very fast like a rocket – can travel as fast as light. Light is the fastest thing in the universe.

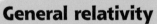

General relativity

Massive things like stars and planets have a lot of gravity that can drag other things closer to them. Einstein explained how this works. As a result, we have a much better understanding of how things move in space.

Light speed

Light travels at around 300,000 kilometres a second. This is the fastest speed in the universe.

One of the most amazing things about Einstein is that he wasn't working at a university when he started making his discoveries. He tried to get a university job but no one would take him. Instead, Einstein found work in an office. His first big idea, special relativity, was developed in his spare time!

Einstein became well known for special relativity, and this helped him get a job at the University of Zurich in Switzerland. In 1913, he moved to the University of Berlin in Germany.

Einstein did not agree with the First World War (1914–1918). He believed that disagreements should be worked out peacefully, and he didn't sign up to be a soldier. Instead, he kept working on his second big idea, general relativity.

In 1921, Einstein won a Nobel Prize for his theories. That is the biggest prize in the world for scientific discoveries!

part of the Nobel Prize is a gold-plated medal

Albert Einstein in his office at the University of Berlin, 1920

Adolf Hilter became the leader of Germany in 1933. Hitler was the head of the Nazi Party. He quickly became a powerful **dictator**. Anyone who disagreed with him was put in prison or killed.

Einstein was a Jew. Hitler hated Jewish people, and he went on to kill huge numbers of Jews during the Second World War (1939–1945). Einstein criticised Hitler, even though this put him in danger.

Einstein wasn't safe in Germany with Hitler in power. He moved to the US in 1933 to continue his work. He never returned to Germany, the country where he was born.

Einstein became a professor at Princeton University in the US. He continued to work on new ideas.

Einstein died in 1955, having never lost his fascination with science. In the years that followed Einstein's death, other scientists built on his ideas to make lots of other discoveries.

Albert Einstein at Princeton University

In 1999, Einstein was named "Person of the Century" by *Time* magazine.

Albert Einstein's ideas have helped us to understand the way the universe works. They have taught us lots of interesting things, especially about space, time and gravity.

Not many people can figure out the complicated maths behind his ideas. But this didn't stop Einstein from being famous in his own lifetime!

CHAPTER 2
Planets and stars

Cecilia Payne-Gaposchkin

Albert Einstein inspired many scientists over the last century. One was Cecilia Payne-Gaposchkin, a young English woman. Payne-Gaposchkin was born in 1900. She didn't have many chances to study science as a child.

Payne-Gaposchkin was a child during the Edwardian period (1901–1910). Edwardian girls were not expected to become scientists – they were expected to get married, have children and look after the home. In the early 1900s, women didn't have the same rights as men. They weren't allowed to vote in national elections or to work in most jobs.

Edwardian schools

Children in Edwardian schools learnt the "three Rs": reading, writing and arithmetic, along with exercise and religious studies. Girls were also taught to sew, mend and cook, to prepare them for looking after a home.

Boys were expected to get jobs and university places were usually only available to boys. Most girls were forced to give up their studies after school. Payne-Gaposchkin was determined to go to university.

a schoolroom in 1905

Payne-Gaposchkin went to study natural science at Cambridge University in 1919. At that time, only a small number of women were able to take university courses in England. Even those who got in were not treated the same as men. In Cambridge, women weren't granted degrees until 1948. They weren't allowed to do complicated research. They weren't expected to become scientists.

Degrees

A degree is an award given to a student who has finished their studies at university. You need a university degree in order to work as a doctor or a teacher.

While she was studying at Cambridge, Payne-Gaposchkin went to a talk about Einstein's ideas on general relativity. She was very excited! She wanted to be an astronomer and learn more about space. This inspired her to move to Radcliffe College, which was linked to Harvard University in the US. There she worked at the Harvard Observatory, a building that was made for the study of stars and planets.

Astronomy

Astronomy is the science of space. It looks at the way that planets, stars and the universe behave. An "astronomer" is a space scientist.

In 1925, Payne-Gaposchkin finished her studies. She had been looking at light that came from different kinds of stars. At that time, everyone believed that stars and planets were made of the same stuff. Payne realised that this was wrong.

What stars are made of

Payne-Gaposchkin realised that planets and stars are not made of the same stuff. Stars are mostly made of gases like hydrogen and helium. Planets are made of a mix of materials. For example, the rock-based planets, like Earth, contain metals like iron and aluminium.

Payne-Gaposchkin realised that hydrogen was the most common thing in the universe. It is present in millions, or even billions, of stars!

Other scientists didn't believe Payne-Gaposchkin. Even at Harvard – one of the few places where women could study for a degree in science – women weren't allowed to become professors. Payne's work wasn't taken seriously. A senior astronomer insisted that she was wrong and that planets and stars were made of the same stuff.

Unlike Einstein, Payne-Gaposchkin didn't win a Nobel Prize or become famous during her lifetime. As a woman, she wasn't able to become an astronomy professor. So instead, she got a job in the observatory, helping to check that the equipment was working.

Payne-Gaposchkin was not the only woman at Harvard whose work was overlooked. Henrietta Swan Leavitt also made important discoveries in the observatory.

Observatory, Harvard College, 1900

Henrietta Swan Leavitt

Henrietta Swan Leavitt was also based at the observatory at Harvard. She worked there until she died in 1921, not long before Payne-Gaposchkin's arrival. Swan Leavitt's discoveries allowed astronomers to work out the distance between stars and Earth. She was never rewarded for her discoveries. But now she is known as "the woman who discovered how to measure the universe".

Four years after Payne-Gaposchkin finished her degree, the senior astronomer who had disagreed with her realised that he had made a mistake. He wrote that stars and planets were made of different elements. Although he mentioned Payne-Gaposchkin's research, he got the credit for the discovery.

In 1938, 13 years after she finished her degree, Payne-Gaposchkin was finally given a research job at Harvard. At last, in 1956, she became a professor and the first female head of the astronomy department.

Payne-Gaposchkin's work on stars changed the study of astronomy. We now understand that stars are huge balls of burning gas and dust, quite different from planets.

We know that they are mostly made of hydrogen, and that hydrogen is the most common gas in the universe. And this knowledge is thanks to Cecilia Payne-Gaposchkin, who never stopped searching for answers.

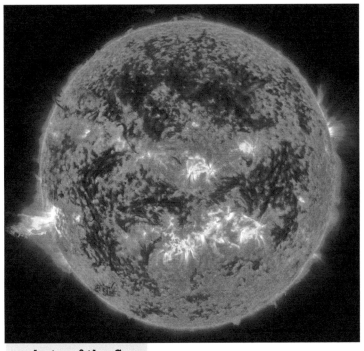

a photo of the Sun

Bonus

The most powerful telescope in the world!

The James Webb Telescope is the world's largest and most powerful space telescope.

It was launched into space by NASA in 2021.

the James Webb Telescope under construction

the James Webb Telescope in space

a **nebula** photographed by
the James Webb Telescope

CHAPTER 3
The evolution of stars

Subrahmanyan Chandrasekhar

Subrahmanyan Chandrasekhar – known as "Chandra" – was born in Lahore in India which is now in modern-day Pakistan. He was born in 1910, around the time that Albert Einstein was working on different theories of relativity.

Chandra was one of ten children. His father was a government officer. His mother translated stories. Chandra's parents and tutors taught him at home until the age of 12. After that, he went to school until he was 15. Chandra started studying for a degree after leaving school. He went to study at the University of Cambridge in the UK.

Chandra was interested in astronomy and the science of stars. In the 1930s, space scientists believed that every star – including our Sun – would eventually lose its gas and become a "white dwarf", a small, dense star that is very, very hot.

In time, the white dwarf would cool down. Scientists believed these cooled white dwarfs would then become black dwarfs that could barely be seen against the blackness of space. The universe isn't old enough yet for black dwarfs to have formed, so it's impossible to know if this is actually true!

It didn't matter whether the star started off large or small – it would always turn into a white dwarf, and then a black dwarf. Or at least, that's what people thought.

At the age of only 19, using Albert Einstein's ideas about general relativity, Chandra made a discovery: giant stars did not act like smaller stars!

The death of a star

Chandra discovered that although most stars turn into white dwarfs, massive stars don't do this. To become a white dwarf, a star must be under a certain size.

White dwarfs: fact file

- White dwarfs are old stars that have run out of gas to burn.
- They are small and dense compared with younger stars.
- Most stars in the Milky Way will eventually become white dwarfs.
- White dwarfs are hotter but dimmer than younger stars.

Our own Sun will eventually become a white dwarf, but don't worry – that won't happen for many millions of years!

So, what is a star? A star is "born" when clusters of dust and gas are pulled together by gravity – the force that pulls objects in the universe towards each other. Bits left over from the star turn into planets that **orbit** the star, just as Earth and the other planets in our **solar system** orbit the Sun.

the Carina Nebula

Regular stars, like our Sun, shine because they burn gases like hydrogen. Once they run out of hydrogen to burn, they turn into red giants. They swell in size and look more red. They carry on burning other gases.

As the star runs out of other gases to burn, it will shrink down to become a white dwarf.

a white dwarf star

the Southern Ring Nebula

Scientists believe that when white dwarfs cool down and lose their energy, they will turn into black dwarfs. This process takes billions of years, so only time will tell if the scientists are correct.

Chandra spent time at European universities researching what happens to stars, from a star's "birth" until it finally fades away. In 1937, he moved to the University of Chicago in the US where he continued his work in astronomy. In 1983, he was awarded the Nobel Prize – the same important award that Albert Einstein had received years before him.

Chandra didn't work out what happened to giant stars that were too big to become white dwarfs.

But in identifying a size factor for stars, he set the stage for more work in this area.

Because of Chandra's research, later scientists learnt that giant stars called "supernovas" don't simply "burn away" over millions or billions of years, like smaller stars. Instead, they explode and turn into neutron stars or black holes!

the Calabash Nebula

Neutron stars

These are very small but very dense stars. For their size, they are the heaviest stars in the universe. A neutron star the size of a teaspoon of sugar would weigh six billion tons!

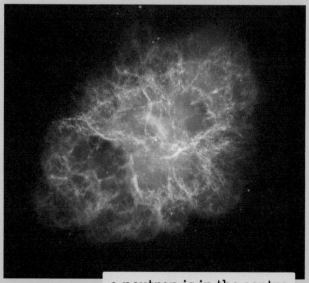

a neutron is in the centre of this nebula

As far back as 1783, an Englishman called John Michell guessed that black holes must exist. But where do black holes come from? What *causes* black holes?

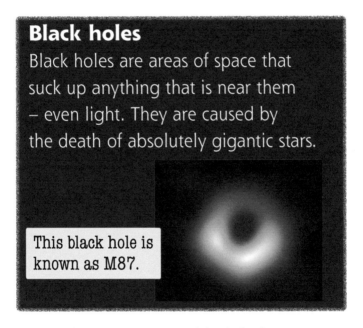

Black holes

Black holes are areas of space that suck up anything that is near them – even light. They are caused by the death of absolutely gigantic stars.

This black hole is known as M87.

Luckily, there are no black holes anywhere near Earth!

Chandra is still famous in astronomy. Stars that are too big to turn into white dwarfs are known as being above the "Chandrasekhar limit". Those stars will eventually become neutron stars or black dwarfs. Smaller stars, like our Sun, are below the Chandrasekhar limit. They will eventually become white dwarfs.

A major telescope was called "Chandra" in Chandra's honour! The Chandra telescope is a spacecraft that moves around space, giving us lots of important information about stars and planets. In this way, long after his death, we still have a lot to learn from Subrahmanyan Chandrasekhar.

the Chandra X-ray Observatory

an X-ray image of deep space
taken by the Chandra telescope

Life cycle of a star

Stars like our Sun don't just "appear" – they develop over millions or even billions of years, gradually changing through time.

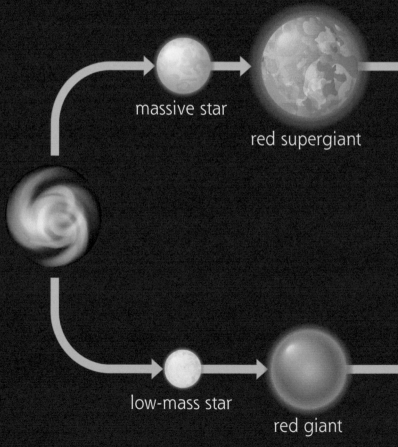

massive star

red supergiant

low-mass star

red giant

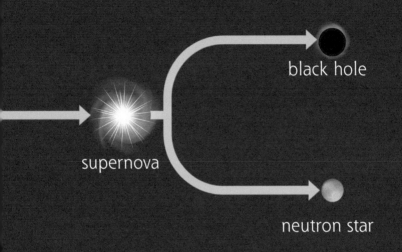

black hole

supernova

neutron star

white dwarf

black dwarf

CHAPTER 4
Travels in space

In the 1950s and 1960s, the US and the Soviet Union were involved in a "space race". They each wanted to show that they were the strongest. So, they both spent a lot of money trying to be the first to send humans to outer space.

The Soviet Union
The Soviet Union was a large group of countries, including Russia.

Katherine Johnson

Katherine Johnson was born in the US in 1918. At that time, Black people were not treated equally to white people. As a Black girl growing up in the South of the US, she was not expected to go to college or university. But Johnson was a very talented student, particularly when it came to maths.

Johnson did so well at school that she was ready to go to college at 15 years old! She finished her college course with the highest possible score, and went on to teach maths to black students. She hoped to inspire her love of maths in her students.

After teaching for a while, Johnson got a chance to go to West Virginia University. She was one of the first three Black students to study at the university – and the very first Black woman! In 1953, Johnson got a job with the US government, for the department that became known as "NASA". She was hired for her excellent maths skills.

NASA

NASA stands for
the National Aeronautics
and Space Administration.
It carries out research and
space travel for the US government.

Johnson helped the US government in its "space race" against the Soviet Union. At this time, the computers that we are used to now hadn't been invented. So Johnson worked as a "human computer", figuring out the complicated maths of space travel.

She was part of a large team of Black women who had the job of working out the distances and speed for different space missions. They used maths to work out what would happen to rockets during space travel, to make sure spaceflights would run smoothly.

A human in space

In 1957, the Soviet Union launched the first spacecraft into space. It was called Sputnik 1 and it was about the size of a beach ball! It took only 98 minutes to orbit Earth.

Sputnik 1 was the first real success of the space race. Other spaceships followed. Some were built to take animals like tortoises and dogs, but no humans had travelled into outer space, until 1961 ...

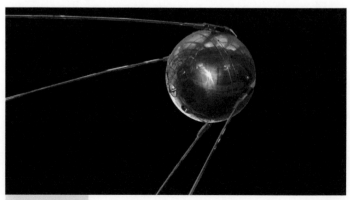

Sputnik 1

On 12th April 1961, a Soviet astronaut called Yuri Gagarin was the first human to go into outer space on a craft called Vostok 1. Gagarin orbited Earth before safely returning to land. It was a space triumph! But the race wasn't over …

Yuri Gagarin in Vostok 1

Back in the US, Johnson's team were making plans for their first human spaceflight. In 1960, a year before Gagarin's space mission, Johnson **co-wrote** a report that set out the complicated maths of flying and landing a spaceship. It was the first time a woman at NASA received any credit for being the author of a research report.

Johnson worked out the maths for the first human spaceflight in the US, Freedom 7. Less than a month after Vostok 1's famous flight, Freedom 7 successfully took astronaut Alan Shepard to space on 5th May 1961. The spacecraft orbited Earth for 15 minutes.

Johnson also checked the calculations for later missions, making sure that they were correct.

The Moon landing

Johnson worked on many space missions during the space race, but she is probably most famous for her work on Apollo 11: the first spaceflight to land on the Moon. Johnson was part of a team of Black women who calculated the direction of the flight, the complicated Moon landing and the return journey.

Apollo 11 rocket

Apollo 11 set off on 16th July 1969 with three astronauts: Neil Armstrong, Michael Collins and Buzz Aldrin. Neil Armstrong was the first person to set foot on the Moon. He was watched on TV by millions of people around the world!

astronaut Buzz Aldrin steps onto the surface of the Moon

Between 1969 and 1972, ten more astronauts landed on the Moon. The astronauts were treated as heroes, especially Neil Armstrong.

Johnson's calculations were of huge importance for the Moon landings. But unlike the male astronauts on the spaceships, hardly anyone knew about her work.

Johnson died on 24th February 2020, aged 101. Before she died, she received an important medal from President Barack Obama. A special computing research centre was opened by NASA in her honour. Even a Hollywood film has been made about her! Now lots of people know Katherine Johnson's role in the history of space travel.

Bonus

Meet the women who put men on the Moon

Two other "human computers" at NASA were key to calculating the maths behind the Moon landing with Katherine Johnson. They were:

Dorothy Vaughan

- Born in Missouri, US
- Dorothy became an expert at a language created specifically for computers!

Mary Jackson
- Born in Virginia, US
- Mary became the first Black female engineer to work at NASA

CHAPTER 5
Deep space

Over the last 100 years, Albert Einstein's general theory of relativity has had a large effect on space science. As we have seen, astronomers like Cecilia Payne-Gaposchkin and Subrahmanyan Chandrasekhar were inspired by Einstein.

General relativity is a theory of huge things like stars and planets. At the same time, other people were developing the science of very small things: the science of atoms, known as "quantum mechanics". Usually, these two types of science did not meet.

Stephen Hawking

Stephen Hawking changed that. He used the science of the very large and the very small to learn more about black holes.

Hawking was born in England in 1942. Unlike the other scientists in this book, he didn't do especially well at school.

His teachers didn't realise how clever he was! But he was always keen to understand how things worked. Hawking's classmates noticed, calling him "Einstein" as a nickname.

Hawking wanted to understand the universe. As a child, he looked for answers to the "big questions". He continued to look for these answers as an adult.

Where do black holes come from?

What caused the big bang?

Is there life on other planets?

Does the universe go on forever?

Hawking studied at the University of Oxford and then the University of Cambridge. In the early 1960s, he found out that he had motor neurone disease.

As Hawking's legs became weaker, he needed to walk with a stick. Eventually, he had to use a special wheelchair in order to get around.

Motor neurone disease

A rare disease that makes the brain and nerves of the body grow weaker. Doctors don't know what causes motor neurone disease.

Motor neurone disease made it easier for Hawking to catch other illnesses. He became unwell while travelling, and had an operation that saved his life but left him without a natural speaking voice. He had to use a machine so that people could understand him. But he didn't stop working.

Hawking was particularly interested in black holes. Black holes are areas of space that suck up any objects that are near them. That means that nothing can escape a black hole – doesn't it?

No human spacecraft can get anywhere near a black hole. But if it could, it would be safe as long as it stayed outside the "event horizon". This is the part of space around the black hole where nothing can escape (not even light!).

If the spaceship travelled beyond
the event horizon, the immense gravity of
the black hole would suck it in!

Hawking's idea

Hawking was surprised to discover that something could escape a black hole's event horizon, while everything else is sucked up. He realised that tiny **particles** can leak out of a black hole.

At first, a lot of people disagreed with Hawking's theory. It seemed to go against the laws of science! But over time, other scientists agreed with him.

This meant that Hawking was successfully able to mix two very different types of scientific rules – the science of the very large, and the science of the very small.

If black holes are, invisible how do we know they are there?

Black holes: fact file

- Some objects in space orbit black holes. A star that seems to orbit "nothing" may actually be orbiting a black hole.

- Black holes suck things towards them. If objects in space seem to be "dragged" in a certain direction, that could mean there's a black hole.

- It's sometimes possible to see "stardust" around a black hole – bits of star that have been torn apart by the black hole.

Hawking continued to work,
even though his health grew worse.
He became well-known as an expert on
the universe. He was often seen on TV and
in newspapers. He met Queen Elizabeth
the Second several times, and won lots of
important prizes.

He wrote several bestselling books where
he shared his excitement about science.
In 2009, Hawking was given a special
award by US President Barack Obama for:

> **persistence and dedication
> [which] has unlocked new
> pathways of discovery and
> inspired everyday citizens.**

The Medal of Freedom ceremony, 2009

Hawking loved to talk about his ideas. He was keen to inspire excitement among people about the big questions of the universe. He travelled whenever he could, and his talks always packed huge rooms as people lined up to see him. He enjoyed trying new and exciting things like travelling into an underground mine and visiting Antarctica.

Stephen Hawking in Antartica, 1997

Stephen Hawking died in Cambridge in 2018, on the same day as Albert Einstein's birthday (14th March). He was 76 years old when he died. He was working right up until the end of his life. His ideas about black holes have helped us to understand the mysteries of space.

Stephen Hawking experiencing weightlessness on a NASA astronaut training plane, in 2007

Bonus

The International Space Station

The International Space Station orbits Earth and allows scientists to carry out important research!

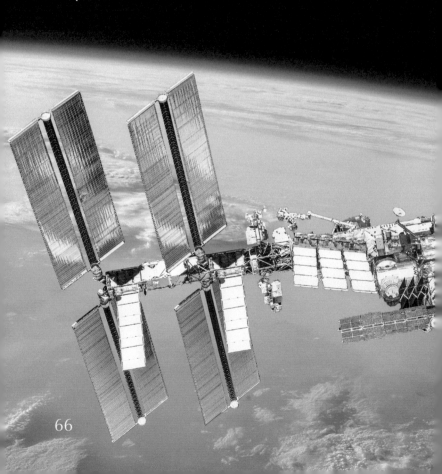

CHAPTER 6
100 years of stargazing

Stars are huge, exploding balls of energy held together by gravity. We know from Cecilia Payne-Gaposchkin that they are full of hydrogen and helium. Stars give off plenty of heat and light, like our own star, the Sun, which warms Earth.

In Chapter 3, we discovered that large stars don't change in the same way as smaller stars. Stars, like our Sun, will eventually shrink into white dwarfs. Huge stars will explode as supernovas either shrink into neutron stars or collapse as black holes.

Jocelyn Bell Burnell

Jocelyn Bell Burnell was born in Northern Ireland in 1943. She was interested in astronomy as a child, and was one of the first girls at her school who was allowed to study science.

Bell Burnell went on to study physics at the University of Glasgow in Scotland. After that, in 1965, she began a research degree in astronomy at the University of Cambridge. It was there that she would make her incredible discovery.

In a field outside Cambridge, Bell Burnell spent time helping to build a special telescope. The telescope was supposed to find signals from outer space. The telescope was attached to a computer, so the researchers could easily print out the information that the telescope found.

Sitting in the muddy field, Bell Burnell looked through pages and pages of information from the telescope. She was searching for "quasars".

Quasars

Quasars are the brightest things in the universe! Most are very, very far away. It's thought that they may be connected to black holes.

an artist's image of a quasar

> **But there are some stars that are different from the rest – they seem to flash on and off.**
> (Jocelyn Bell Burnell)

Jocelyn Bell Burnell at the Mullard Radio Astronomy Observatory, near Cambridge

Bell Burnell noticed something unusual on the pages in front of her. She leafed backwards and forwards. There was a "beat" or a pulse repeated every 1.3 seconds.

Bell Burnell called the senior scientist on the project. He said that if the pulses were regular, they must have been caused by a human-made thing, like electrical equipment – they couldn't be from outer space.

The next day, the senior scientist joined Bell Burnell at the telescope and saw that the pulses were appearing between stars. They *were* coming from outer space!

What Bell Burnell had spotted was something no one had ever seen before. It was a "pulsar".

Pulsars: fact file

- Pulsars are types of neutron stars – small and incredibly dense stars that sometimes form when a massive star dies.

- Pulsars seem to blink on and off, creating a "pulsing" beat.

- In fact, pulsars do not blink off – they are actually spinning very quickly. It's only when their bright light turns towards us that we can see it.

pulsar

A combined image from NASA's Chandra and Spitzer space telescopes. The white point at the centre is a pulsar.

The senior scientist that Bell Burnell was working with won the Nobel Prize in 1974 for his role in discovering pulsars. It was the same top scientific award won by Albert Einstein and Subrahmanyan Chandrasekhar for their discoveries.

Although she was the first one to spot the existence of pulsars, Bell Burnell didn't win the Nobel Prize. As we have seen with Henrietta Swan Leavitt, Cecilia Payne-Gaposchkin and Katherine Johnson, women were not always treated equally to men.

Science is for everyone

Bell Burnell went on to work at universities around the UK. She was made a Dame (the equivalent of being **knighted**) by Queen Elizabeth the Second. She has won many prizes. One of these was the 2018 Special Breakthrough Prize in Fundamental Physics for her discovery of pulsars and her leadership in science. The prize money was three million dollars, which is three times as much as the Nobel Prize!

Over the last 100 years, most space scientists have been men from European backgrounds. It was tough for women to get into science.

Jocelyn Bell Burnell wanted her prize money to make a difference. She donated her winnings to help women become scientists, along with other groups of people who have often been excluded from science. She believes that science is for everyone!

In this book, we have learnt about some of the amazing space science of the last 100 years. We have taken a look at Albert Einstein's ideas and how they changed the way we see the universe. We have found out about white dwarfs, pulsars, neutron stars and black holes. And we have discovered how teams of "human computers", like Katherine Johnson, helped to put people on the Moon.

There's still so much to learn about our universe. So many mysteries remain uncovered. More than ever, we need bright minds to figure out the secrets of space. Could you be a space scientist of the future?

What might *you* discover?

Bonus

Our solar system

Meet the other planets that share our solar system.

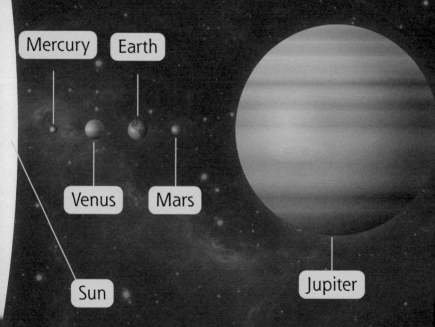

Mercury

Earth

Venus

Mars

Sun

Jupiter

Saturn

Uranus

Neptune

Bonus

What happens at the Space Center?

At the Space Center in Houston, Texas, US, astronauts train for space missions.

At the Space Center, you can see ...

This replica of the command centre from Apollo 11 – the first Moon landing.

astronauts training in simulators of space shuttles

robots and rovers to study the planets being built and tested

the actual space suits used by astronauts on various missions

83

Glossary

co-wrote wrote with another writer

dictator a ruler with complete power

galaxies collections of stars, gas clouds and solar systems held together by gravity

knighted given an honour by a British king or queen for service to their country

nebula a giant cloud of dust and gas in space

orbit a curved path followed by an object going round a planet, moon or star

particles very small pieces

solar system a sun and all the planets, moons and objects in orbit around it

Index

About the author

How did you get into writing?

I loved writing stories when I was a child but I never expected to be an author. I was training to be a lawyer when I started writing my first book, *The Tygrine Cat*.

Inbali Iserles

What do you hope readers will get out of the book?

There are still so many unsolved mysteries about space. I hope this book will encourage readers to push for answers too, just like the incredible scientists in this book. The world needs questioning minds!

Is there anything in this book that relates to your own experiences?

My dad is a maths professor and growing up, our house was full of scientists. I loved asking questions about the mysteries of space. What is the fastest thing in the universe? What are stars made of? If we can't see black holes, how do we know they exist?

Why did you decide to write this book?

Our understanding of outer space has changed a lot in the last 100 years. I wanted to shine a light on a few of the space scientists whose creative thinking and hard work gave us answers to some of the big questions.

Do you have a favourite scientist in the book?

This is a difficult question! Albert Einstein was truly one of a kind, and his ideas about relativity changed the world. But probably my favourite scientist in the book is Jocelyn Bell Burnell. Not only did she discover flashing stars called "pulsars", but she used her success to help women in science.

Would you want to go into space, if you could?

I think it would be magical to travel into that velvety darkness with an orbit or two of our beautiful Earth. It could be so much fun to feel weightless, like astronauts do in zero gravity. But I wouldn't want to go for too long – I would miss my family and friends too much!

What surprised you most when you were researching the book?

Some of the scientists in this book made their biggest discoveries when they were only students, or even in their spare time! Isn't that amazing?

Book chat

What have you learned from reading the book?

If you had to give the book a new title, what would you choose?

Which part of the book surprised you most? Why?

Which of the scientists in the book do you think is the most interesting? Why?

What was the most interesting thing you learnt from reading the book?

If you could ask the author one question, what would it be?

Would you want to go into space? Why or why not?

If you could talk to one scientist from the book, who would you pick? What would you say to them?

Had you heard of any of the scientists before reading this book?

Have you read any other books on space?

Why do you think the book is called Spectacular Space?

What do you think is the most amazing discovery in this book?

Have you ever been
to an observatory?
Would you like to go?

What's the most
spectacular thing
you've ever seen in
the night sky?

Would you be
interested to read
more books on space?

Book challenge:

Go out and try to see some stars in
the night sky! (Can you notice any
different colours?)

Collins
BIG CAT

Published by Collins
An imprint of HarperCollins*Publishers*

The News Building
1 London Bridge Street
London SE1 9GF
UK

Macken House
39/40 Mayor Street Upper
Dublin 1
D01 C9W8
Ireland

Text © Inbali Iserles 2023
Design and illustrations ©
HarperCollins*Publishers* Limited 2023

Inbali Iserles asserts her moral right to be
identified as author of this work.

10 9 8 7 6 5 4 3

ISBN 978-0-00-862483-5

British Library Cataloguing-in-Publication
Data
A catalogue record for this publication is
available from the British Library.

Download the teaching notes and
word cards to accompany this book at:
http://littlewandle.org.uk/signupfluency/

Get the latest Collins Big Cat news at
collins.co.uk/collinsbigcat

Author: Inbali Iserles
Publisher: Lizzie Catford
Product manager and commissioning editor: Caroline Green
Series editor: Charlotte Raby
Development editor: Catherine Baker
Project manager: Emily Hooton
Content editor: Daniela Mora Chavarría
Copyeditor: Sally Byford
Proofreader: Catherine Dakin
Picture researcher: Sophie Hartley
Typesetter: 2Hoots Publishing Services Ltd
Cover designer: Sarah Finan
Production controller: Katharine Willard

Collins would like to thank the teachers and children at the
following schools who took part in the trialling of Big Cat
for Little Wandle Fluency: Burley And Woodhead Church of
England Primary School; Chesterton Primary School; Lady
Margaret Primary School; Little Sutton Primary School;
Parsloes Primary School.

Printed and bound in the UK

MIX
**Paper | Supporting
responsible forestry**
FSC
www.fsc.org **FSC™ C007454**

This book is produced from independently
certified FSC™ paper to ensure
responsible forest management.

For more information visit:
www.harpercollins.co.uk/green

Acknowledgements
The publishers gratefully acknowledge the permission
granted to reproduce the copyright material in this book.
Every effort has been made to trace copyright holders and
to obtain their permission for the use of copyright material.
The publishers will gladly receive any information enabling
them to rectify any error or omission at the first opportunity.

Cover: Geopix/Alamy, p2tl Bettmann/Getty Images, p2tr
& p28 Science History Images/Alamy, p2b PF-(bygone1)/
Alamy, p3tl & p43 NASA, p3tr & p69 PA Images/Alamy, p3b
Sueddeutsche Zeitung Photo/Alamy, p5 titoOnz/Alamy, p6
Alpha Historica/Alamy, p11 Alpha Historica/Alamy, p13
Keystone-France/Getty Images, p15 Science History Images/
Alamy, p17 Pictorial Press Ltd/Alamy, pp20–21 NASA, p22
Glasshouse Images/Alamy, p23 GRANGER – Historical Picture
Archive/Alamy, p25 NASA Photo/Alamy, p32 Luc Novovitch/
Alamy, p33 NASA, ESA, CSA, STSCI/Science Photo Library,
pp34–35 NASA, p36 NASA, p37 EUROPEAN SOUTHERN
OBSERVATORY/EHT COLLABORATION/Science Photo Library,
pp38–39 Geopix/Alamy, p39 Stocktrek Images, Inc./Alamy,
p46 NASA Archive/Alamy, p47 Science History Images/
Alamy, p49 GRANGER - Historical Picture Archive/Alamy,
p50 NASA, p52 NASA Archive/Alamy, p53 NASA Image
Collection/Alamy, p55 Trinity Mirror/ Mirrorpix/Alamy, p63
White House Photo/Alamy, p64 Miguel Sayago/Alamy, p65
Nasa/Science Photo Library, p71 NASA, p72 Daily Herald
Archive/Getty Images, p74–75 NASA, p79 ESA/Hubble &
NASA, p86 © Richard Mansell, all other photos Shutterstock.